02-3362

Adventures in Canadian History

DR. KANE OF THE ARCTIC SEAS

Books for Younger Readers by Pierre Berton

The Golden Trail
The Secret World of Og

ADVENTURES IN CANADIAN HISTORY
The Capture of Detroit
The Death of Isaac Brock
Revenge of the Tribes
Canada Under Siege

Bonanza Gold
The Klondike Stampede
Trails of '98
City of Gold

Parry of the Arctic
Jane Franklin's Obsession
Dr. Kane of the Arctic Seas

The Railway Pathfinders
The Men in Sheepskin Coats
A Prairie Nightmare
Steel Across the Plains

PIERRE BERTON

Exploring the Frozen North

Dr. Kane of the Arctic Seas

ILLUSTRATIONS BY PAUL MC CUSKER

M&S

An M&S Paperback Original from
McClelland & Stewart Inc.
The Canadian Publishers

An M&S Paperback Original from McClelland & Stewart Inc.

First printing January 1993

Canadian Cataloguing in Publication Data

Berton, Pierre, 1920-
Dr. Kane of the Arctic Seas

(Adventures in Canadian history. Exploring the frozen North)
"An M&S paperback original."
Includes index.
ISBN 0-7710-1446-5

1. Kane, Elisha Kent, 1820-1857 – Juvenile literature. 2. Arctic regions – Discovery and exploration – American – Juvenile literature. 3. Canada, Northern – Discovery and exploration – American – Juvenile literature.
4. Explorers – Canada – Biography – Juvenile literature. 5. Explorers – United States – Biography – Juvenile literature. 6. Physicians – United States – Biography – Juvenile literature. I. McCusker, Paul. II. Title. III. Series: Berton, Pierre, 1920-   . Adventures in Canadian history. Exploring the frozen North.

G635.K35B47 1993   919.804′092   C92-095671-8

Series design by Tania Craan
Cover design by Stephen Kenny
Text design by Randolph Rozema
Cover illustration by Scott Cameron
Interior illustrations by Paul McCusker
Maps by James Loates
Editor: Peter Carver

Typesetting by M&S

The support of the Government of Ontario through the Ministry of Culture and Communications is acknowledged.

Printed and bound in Canada
McClelland & Stewart Inc.
The Canadian Publishers
481 University Avenue
Toronto, Ontario
M5G 2E9

CONTENTS

Maps appear on pages 8-9, 30, 44, 66.

The events in this book actually happened as told here. Nothing has been made up. This is a work of non-fiction and there is archival evidence for every story and, indeed, every remark made in this book.

Adventures in Canadian History

Dr. Kane of the Arctic Seas

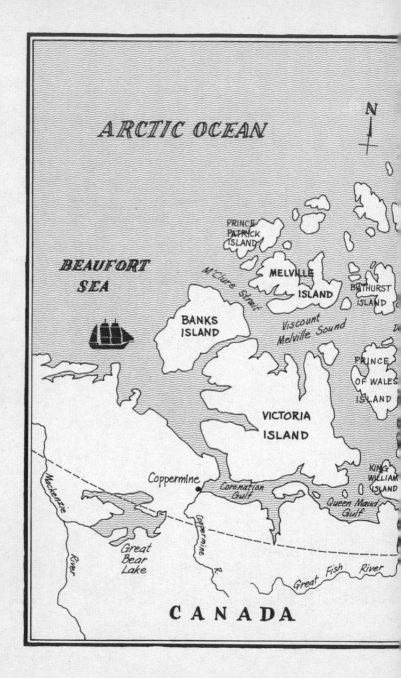

N

ARCTIC OCEAN

BEAUFORT
SEA

PRINCE
PATRICK
ISLAND

MELVILLE
ISLAND

BATHURST
ISLAND

M'Clure Strait

BANKS
ISLAND

Viscount
Melville Sound

PRINCE
OF WALES
ISLAND

VICTORIA
ISLAND

Coppermine

Coronation
Gulf

KING
WILLIAM
ISLAND

Queen Maud
Gulf

Mackenzie

Coppermine R.

Great
Bear
Lake

River

Great Fish River

CANADA

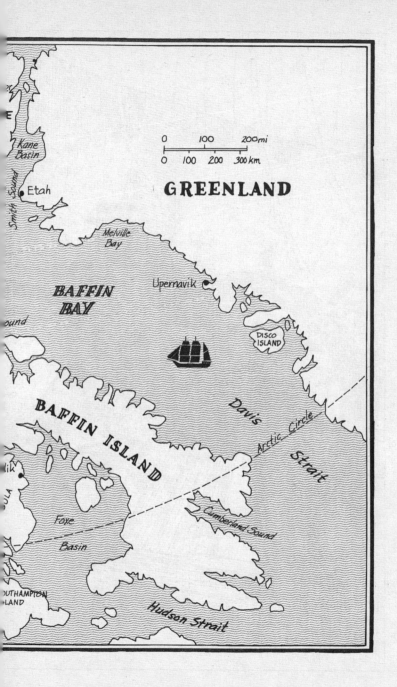

CHAPTER ONE

The invalid

O F ALL THE NINETEENTH century explorers who probed the frozen world of the Canadian Arctic, by far the best known was an ailing, twenty-nine-year-old surgeon, Elisha Kent Kane. He later gave himself the romantic title of "Dr. Kane of the Arctic Seas," and he is all but forgotten now. But there was a time when his memoirs were devoured by thousands of enthusiastic readers.

Kane was his own best publicity agent. Both Roald Amundsen, the conqueror of the North West Passage, and Robert Peary, the polar explorer, were raised on Kane's version of his Arctic adventures. When he returned from his first trip to the Arctic in 1850, his dramatic descriptions of the harsh polar conditions electrified his generation. He was – and remained – a national hero, as much for his ability to tell a good story as for his explorations. By contrast, the British naval men who opened up the Arctic were far more restrained and tight-lipped. It was in their nature to make light of their troubles. As a result, Kane makes livelier reading.

On the face of it, this restless, driven man had no business being in the Arctic. He had a damaged heart and, indeed, would die before the decade was over. As a medical student suffering from rheumatic fever he'd gone to his bed each night never knowing whether he'd wake up the next morning. He was slender and fragile, though very handsome. He was a bit of a rebel who hated the discipline of the Navy. He grew seasick easily. In 1850, on his first expedition to the Arctic, he was so ill his commander tried to send him home. Kane stubbornly refused.

On the other hand, Kane was an adventurer. He had travelled to the ends of the earth – to Mexico, Egypt, the Mediterranean, Brazil, the African coast, the interiors of India and China. In ancient Egypt he had explored the catacombs of Thebes. He had stood at the entrance to the pass at Thermopylae where a handful of Greeks held off a Persian army in the brave days of old. He had hiked across the storied peninsula known to the classical world as the Peloponnesus; and he had once hung suspended from a bamboo rope, attached to the two-hundred-foot (61 m) crag over a volcanic crater in the Philippines.

For much of that time he had been ill. He had contracted "tic fever" in Macao, "coast fever " in Africa, and "congestive typhus" during the Mexican War. In Mexico he was also wounded in the abdomen by a lance during a hand-to-hand combat as the head of a guerrilla company.

Yet he kept on. One of his fellow students was convinced that his chronic heart problem led him to attempt reckless escapades. He would not put up with, he said, "the miserable tediousness of small adventures." Doomed to an early grave, he had nothing to lose. His journal suggests that he was out to prove something, not just to himself, but especially to his father, who had a low opinion of him.

In 1850 the Canadian Arctic was as mysterious as the moon. Two fur-trading explorers, Samuel Hearne and Alexander Mackenzie, had reached the northern tip of the continent in the previous century – but no one knew what lay beyond.

Some believed that the land might extend to the North Pole, for no one had actually explored the coastline. Some felt that another continent lay between North America and the Pole. Some believed in the myth of an "Open Polar Sea" – a warm Mediterranean lying beyond the ice pack. Some believed that the Arctic was wide open, without any land masses; others were convinced (rightly) that it was made up of islands.

For years every seaman had dreamed of a short cut through North America to the fabled Orient, with its silks, spices, and treasures. They gradually realized that if there was such a North West Passage, it would be found somewhere beyond the Arctic mists.

Since the days of Elizabeth I, bold men in wooden ships had sought the elusive passage. But the real search did not begin until the world was at peace after Napoleon's overthrow in 1815. The Royal Navy, having little else to do, decided to map the unknown corners of the world. And so, ship after ship was sent north to explore the Canadian Arctic, and to find the elusive passage, if indeed such a passage did exist.

The British naval men were, by and large, a sensible lot. It must have been obvious to many that such a passage would not be practical. The land to the north was too cold and too remote.

Yet it drew them like a magnet. The idea of a lane of water leading directly to the riches of the East had been fixed in the folk memories of sailors for three centuries. Few could dismiss it from their imaginations.

Besides, whoever found the passage would become a hero, and a wealthy one at that. For the British honoured their heroes – especially their naval heroes – with practical rewards.

This helps to explain why John Franklin, a British naval captain in his 60th year, was eager to seek the passage. He was well past his prime and could easily have retired to a quiet existence in the country, but he couldn't resist the lure of the unknown.

He had already led two land expeditions to map the Canadian Arctic coast. But in 1845 he urged that he be given a chance to lead an expedition even farther north. The naval authorities humoured him, gave him two ships, the *Erebus* and the *Terror,* and sent him off, with great pomp and ceremony, to find the passage.

Franklin and his 129 men vanished into the Arctic. None of them was ever seen alive again, nor was there any real hint of what had happened. He and his ships seem to have been swallowed up as surely as if they had been devoured by some carnivorous sea beast.

The mystery of Franklin's fate aroused all of Europe into the most massive search in history. Eventually, other nations took part in a quest that occupied almost fifteen years.

Because no one knew where Franklin was, the frozen world was scoured from the western tip of Russian Alaska to its eastern entrance at Lancaster Sound. As a result, the Arctic was opened up, the islands mapped, the lanes of water charted, and Canada's boundaries stretched north to the Pole itself.

The Americans entered the search in 1850, years after Franklin's disappearance. Henry Grinnell, a wealthy New York shipping magnate, egged on by Franklin's wife, Jane, (see *Jane Franklin's Obsession* in this series) bought two ships and sent them north to help the British. Elisha Kent Kane was eager to go along and signed on as chief medical officer.

Kane was as eager to go north as Franklin had been. These were years of high adventure and the Arctic held no terror for a man who had tempted a Philippine volcano. The Arctic itself had never known such activity. In 1850 when the Grinnell expedition headed north, no fewer than nine British ships were fitted out to take part in the search. Only one got back that year, while the other eight were imprisoned in the ice, their sledging parties fanning out in a fruitless hunt for the lost explorers.

Kane and members of the Grinnell expedition examine traces of the lost Franklin expedition.

Grinnell turned both his vessels, the *Advance* and the smaller *Rescue,* over to the United States government so that their crews might be placed under naval discipline. By August the expedition had reached Greenland and (while Kane fought seasickness) set off for Lancaster Sound in the heart of the Arctic. Most of the British ships were concentrated in that area and here the first clues to the Franklin puzzle were discovered.

Turning north up Wellington Channel, the searchers found what appeared to be a Royal Navy encampment on little Beechey Island. It was the first sign that Franklin had come this way. Kane was eager to inspect these early traces — circular mounds of limestone marking the position of tents, a crude fireplace, some bird bones, the rusting top of a food canister, and a few scraps of canvas.

Here they also came upon the graves of three of Franklin's men who had died in the first winter of his exploration. There could be no doubt that this was the site of Franklin's first winter camp. But where had he gone after that? No one really knew.

To avoid getting trapped by the freeze-up, all the ships were forced to move out to more open water. With masses of new ice groaning and grating her sides, the *Advance* struggled past ice tables fourteen feet (4.3 m) thick and hummocks that resembled cones of crushed sugar forty feet (12 m) high. Unlike the British, the Americans had no intention of wintering in the Arctic. It was time to return home.

Unfortunately, the smaller *Rescue* had become separated from her sister ship. She would have to be found before both were imprisoned by the ice.

"We're literally running for our lives," Kane wrote in his journal. "We're staggering along under all sail, forcing our way while we can." It was now so cold that coffee froze in the mugs.

At last the missing ship was found far to the west, sheltered by the cliffs of Griffith Island in Barrow Strait. The *Advance* took her in tow. Now the two little vessels headed eastward in a race against time and weather, leaving their British comrades behind.

Kane could hear the sounds of his own ship crunching through the new ice like a "rasping noise of close-grain sugar." His limbs grew stiff as he tried to warm them in his tiny cabin. And then the worst happened: the ice caught them. They were frozen in for the winter – "glued up," in Kane's phrase, at the mouth of Wellington Channel.

They were helpless – prisoners of the shifting ice pack. For the next two months the ice pushed them north into unexplored waters. Then it pushed them back again past their starting point. All around them, in their icy cradle, the roar of the surging pack rang in their ears, "a wild, yet not unmusical chorus," in Kane's description. It was almost as if the ice were alive, he thought, uttering animal-like shrieks or plaintive cries like those of a nighthawk.

The two little vessels were not equipped to ward off the stinging cold. As the winter advanced it grew fiercer. Food froze. No one had experienced cold as vicious as this, even in the chilly regions of the American Midwest. Barrels of fruit had to be chopped apart with an axe. Sauerkraut was as hard as rock. Butter and lard had to be carved with a cold chisel and mallet. When one seaman tried to bite into an icicle, a piece of it froze to his tongue. Two others lost all the skin on their lips. Facial hair turned to cardboard. If a man stuck out his tongue, it froze to his beard.

They feared to walk too far from the ship over the broken ice. Kane felt that the frost extended to his brain. A strange weariness fell over the crew whose members were infected by a desire to sit down and rest. Knowing that drowsiness and death could easily follow, they kept on their feet.

The men's features turned a ghastly white. Morale began to drop. It required an effort even to wash. At Christmas they put on a play and attempted a footrace. The effort exhausted them. One man actually fainted. Now the telltale signs of scurvy appeared – a swelling of the gums, soreness in the joints, fatigue. Simply climbing a ladder caused the strongest man to pant for breath.

"I long for the light," Kane wrote in his journal. "Dear, dear sun, no wonder you are worshipped!"

The crew of the *Rescue* was forced to abandon their ship which had been badly battered by the ice. They crowded aboard the *Advance* – thirty-three men jammed into a room no bigger than Kane's father's library in Philadelphia. For them, there was no privacy.

On January 29, after eighty-six days of total darkness, the sun came back at last and the crew gave three hearty cheers. Kane did not take part. Instead he found a hummock of ice a mile (1.6 km) from the ship where he could drink in the rosy light of dawn by himself. "Never, till the grave-sod of the ice cover me, may I forego this blessing of blessings again!" he wrote dramatically.

By February 10, the two ships – one crammed with thirty-three men, the other empty, drifting beside it – had been carried more than three hundred miles (480 km). Kane felt the scurvy in his limbs. It was as if he had taken a bad beating. Nineteen men now suffered from ulcerated gums. The worst were those who had eaten salt meat and hardtack without vegetables. Kane tried to treat this vitamin deficiency with olive oil and lime juice and those that took his advice began to get well.

March arrived. The *Advance* was still locked in the ice. A group of seamen went across to the *Rescue* and dug an eight foot (2.4 m) pit around her hull so she might be repaired – a novel kind of dry dock. Then the first open leads of water appeared. In April the *Rescue*'s crew returned to their ship. On June 5 the breakup came so suddenly the men had to scramble to reload the ships.

Seated on the deck of the *Advance,* Kane saw a wondrous spectacle before him. A series of frozen waves seemed to be rippling across the white expanse. This astonishing spectacle – a seemingly solid surface swelling, rising, and falling, made him feel a bit seasick. Now the icebergs began to break up, shifting away to form a stream of moving ice.

The *Advance* was still attached to a submerged mattress of ice. The captain anchored a cable to an iceberg and let the swell of the water drive it against the ship like a great battering ram. Finally, after eight months and twenty-four days, they were free at last.

They had not found what they were searching for. Sir John Franklin and his crew were still missing. When they returned to New York on September 7, it was to report defeat.

CHAPTER TWO

~

The spirit rappers

ELISHA KENT KANE was determined to return north. He had become obsessed by the idea of Arctic exploration. However, another obsession had also captured him – one of the strangest to which any Arctic explorer had succumbed. He had fallen head over heels in love with an extraordinary nineteen-year-old named Margaret Fox, who was as famous in her own way as the Arctic hero. Some thought her close to being a saint. Others saw her as a mystic. A few thought she was a servant of the devil. A few were convinced she was a fraud.

For Margaret Fox was a medium, a "spirit rapper," who communicated, so it was said, with the souls of the dead. They rapped out messages from the spirit world using a simple code of numbers – one rap for "A", two for "B", and so on. Margaret and her younger sister Katherine were, indeed, the first of their kind – the model for all future mediums. For the cult of spiritualism began with the Fox sisters in 1848.

By the time Kane discovered the two sisters during their

Philadelphia performance in November, 1852, the craze had swept the nation. One million people believed in it. What started as a popular social fad had been transformed into a religious movement.

The nation was captivated by these innocent-looking young women, with their dark, lustrous eyes, their solemn features, and their remarkable clear skin, which gave them an other-worldly look. People tried to prove they were frauds but that only added to their appeal.

The two sisters sat at the séance tables with their hands and arms unconcealed, while the "spirits" spelled out the answers to questions thrown at them. Even when they were stripped of their clothing, as happened once, the rappings continued.

These "Rochester Rappings," as they were called, had begun at the Fox home near Rochester, New York, in 1848. The two girls – Katherine was then thirteen, Margaret sixteen – had scared their mother out of her wits when these mysterious sounds had appeared, apparently from nowhere. The girls had merely intended to tease their parents. But the results were so startling it got beyond control before they could reveal their secret. Nor did they confess it for another forty years.

The trick was very simple: the sisters both had double-jointed toes, which they learned to crack with little effort. And so, on this flimsy foundation, modern spiritualism was born – largely as the result of the exploitation of the two teenage girls by their older, widowed sister, Leah.

Kane pays a visit to his beloved Margaret Fox and her mother.

Kane did not believe in spirit rappings. He had dropped in on the sisters at the Union Hotel in Philadelphia out of sheer curiosity. When he saw Margaret reading by the window, she seemed so innocent that he thought he had knocked on the wrong door. It appears to have been a case of love at first sight.

His letters, later published after his death, suggest his passion: "I am sick … sick with hard work, and with nobody to nurse or care for me … is it any wonder that I long to look — only to look — at that dear little deceitful mouth of yours; to feel your hair tumbling over my cheeks.…"

But there was the problem of the spirit rappings. Kane was convinced that Margaret was living a life of deception. Even as he planned his next assault on the Arctic, he tried to convince her to change her way of life.

"When I think of you dear darling, wasting your time and youth and conscience for a few paltry dollars and think of the crowds who come nightly to hear of the wild stories of the frozen north, I sometimes feel that we are not removed after all. My brain and your body are each the sources of attraction and I confess there is not so much difference," he wrote.

There were, of course, vast differences. She was an uneducated teenager, one of six children from the poverty-stricken family of an alcoholic. She didn't really know what she was doing and made no claims of any kind. He was an educated, well-travelled, and snobbish member of a prominent Philadelphia family. He longed to marry her. His family opposed it.

Throughout his life Kane had vainly sought his father's approval. Now his father wanted him to marry a wealthy Philadelphia girl. But Kane was in love with Margaret Fox. As far as Philadelphia society was concerned, she was the most unsuitable of all possible wives. It wasn't only that she was a notorious stage performer; there was also the matter of her upbringing.

So Kane decided he would change Margaret. He would go off to the Arctic, she would give up spirit rapping and, at his expense, enter a boarding school of his choosing far from the temptations of the big cities.

That did not sit well with Leah, the elder sister, who was making money from the séances. But Kane was firm: "Your life is worse than tedious, it is sinful, and that you have so long resisted its temptation shows me that you were born for better things than to entertain strangers at a dollar a head."

Meanwhile, during these winter months he was scribbling away on a book about his Arctic adventures and dashing from city to city delivering lectures. No wonder that in February and again in April he fell ill from the rheumatic fever that had weakened his heart.

Planning for the new Arctic expedition went on without him. Once again he would take the *Advance* – the ship from the previous expedition. But this would be a private venture; the U.S. Navy would only supply seamen. Fortunately, Henry Grinnell, the wealthy Arctic enthusiast who had provided funds for the first expedition, came up with more money.

In addition to the boats and sledges, pemmican and pickles, books and biscuits that were part of the expedition's supplies, Kane arranged for a more personal item. He paid an Italian painter to make a portrait of Margaret to take with him on the voyage, which was set for May.

With that done, he had her spirited away to a tiny village eighteen miles (29 km) from Philadelphia. There she was to receive an education from the wife of the local miller. That reduced her to tears, but Kane in one last letter attempted to comfort her:

"The day will come," he wrote "– bright as sunshine on the waters – when I claim your hand and unrestrained by the trammels of our mutual dread, live with you in peace, tranquillity and affection.

"Be good and pure. Restrain every thought which interferes with a guileless life, and live to prove your improvement, your love for – Ky."

CHAPTER THREE

The "Open Polar Sea"

A S HE PREPARED FOR HIS expedition, Kane kept insisting his main purpose was to search for Franklin.

He pretended to believe that Franklin and his lost crews were somewhere on the lost shores of the Open Polar Sea, living off its animal life, but unable to leave their hunting grounds and cross the frozen desert which was said to lie between the Open Polar Sea and the rest of the world.

Many of the explorers of that day were convinced, against all reason, that an "Open Polar Sea," as they called it, lay beyond the barrier of ice that blocked the way to the North Pole. According to this theory, a vast Arctic lake of still water lay somewhere beyond Smith Sound in the High Arctic. Here, so it was said, the air was milder and skies free of icy blasts. Kane saw this as a kind of Mediterranean. It was his intention to head for Smith Sound and try to break into the mysterious sea.

There was, of course, no Open Polar Sea. Like many of his colleagues, Kane was a victim of wishful thinking. It was pleasant to believe that somewhere, far to the north, the ice would vanish and the climate grow milder. But there wasn't a shred of evidence to support that belief – quite the opposite. Why would the ice suddenly melt as the Pole grew nearer? What would make the northern climate suddenly put on a southern face?

Kane's plan was to advance into the unknown by dogsled until he reached the mysterious sea. Then he would launch small boats and set out upon its waters. And so, on May 31, with a company of seventeen officers and men, and with crowds cheering and guns booming, he set off, declaring that "neither silence nor the vain glory of attaining an unreached North shall divert me from this one conscientious aim...."

Was that his real purpose? One wonders. Kane knew that another explorer, a British naval officer, Commander Edward Inglefield, had already covered the territory he was heading for and found no clue of the missing Franklin expedition. It is likely that he was simply using the Franklin mystery as an excuse to raise funds for another discovery. While pretending to look for the lost expedition he gave every sign of seeking something even more difficult to reach – the North Pole itself.

When the *Advance* set sail from New York on May 31, 1853, Kane had not yet recovered entirely from his bout of rheumatic fever. He was also violently seasick as the little one hundred and forty-four-ton (128 tonne) brig (a two-masted, square-rigged ship) tossed and rolled in the Atlantic. The slightest swell made him ill. Hardly anybody in the crew of seventeen thought he would recover. But recover he did.

It was not a very encouraging start for a man who had never before captained a ship, who knew little of navigation, and wasn't used to being a leader. He had little shipboard experience because in previous journeys as a doctor he had confined himself to the care of the sick. But now he found himself in command of a strange crew who had never worked together before. Many were amateurs and at least two were troublemakers.

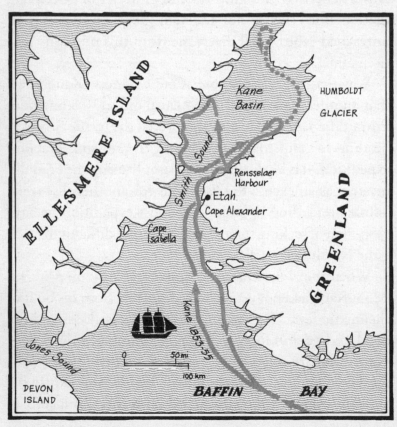

Kane's search for Franklin and the North Pole, 1853-55.

One of these ruffians was a harbour boatman from the city's turbulent east side, named William Godfrey. The other was called John Hussey, but his real name was John Blake. Both of them would cause a great deal of trouble long before the expedition reached its goal.

On July 20, the ship reached Upernavik, the farthest north of the west Greenland settlements, well to the south of Melville Bay. Kane took on two new crew members – a plump and cheerful Inuit youth of nineteen, Hans Christian Hendrik, and Carl Petersen, a Danish dog driver who had considerable Arctic experience.

Petersen came reluctantly. He wasn't impressed by the expedition or by Kane or by his sailing master, John Wall Wilson, who knew nothing about ice. The crew was untrained – only the carpenter, Charles Ohlsen, had any real experience in polar navigation. And the food was inadequate; there were no fresh provisions – only salt meat.

Kane plunged ahead with all the enthusiasm of an amateur. In doing so he collided with a huge iceberg, losing a boat and jib boom. He blundered on through the middle ice of Baffin Bay until on August 6 he saw two huge fifteen-hundred-foot (457 m) capes – Alexander and Isabella – that formed the gateways to Smith Sound.

Godfrey and Blake were causing trouble. Godfrey was imprisoned for assaulting the sailing master, Wilson. But Kane couldn't keep him captive because he needed every man on deck.

He sailed through the great basin that today bears his

name. By this time he had gone farther north than any other white man. But winter was closing in and the crew, exhausted from forcing the ship through the ice, was uneasy and homesick. They wanted to go back. Kane wanted to plunge forward.

In the end his officers persuaded him to stop. He couldn't go back because the ice was closing in, so he found a sheltered bay on the Greenland shore. He named it Rensselaer Harbour after his father's country estate. There he prepared to spend the gloomiest winter any of them had ever known.

Except for the people of Spitzbergen, north of Norway, warmed by a milder current, no white man had ever wintered this far north. They faced a gloomy winter. Even the pugnacious Godfrey was troubled by "blue devils." The unchanging polar landscape, he later wrote, was such that "the very soul of man seems to be suffocated by the oppressive gloom." Hans, the Inuit, was frightened to the point of weeping – homesick for his sweetheart. He tried to leave but Kane talked him out of it.

It was more than the polar darkness that cast a pall over the company. The men shivered in their quarters, eating cold food because Kane hadn't estimated the right amount of fuel for the journey. By the end of February they were out of oil, almost out of candles, and rapidly running out of coal. It wasn't possible to melt enough water in which to wash. They had to give up their tea. There was no more fresh bread. The galley stove was abandoned and all cooking done in the smoky main cabin.

Kane's own personality made things worse. The man who had portrayed himself in his memoirs as a selfless hero turned out to be snobbish, overbearing, boastful, and quite unable to keep his crew in order. Wilson thought him "peevish, coarse, sometimes insulting … the most self-conceited man I ever saw." By January the officers were eating their meals in silence to avoid a tongue-lashing from their captain.

By mid-winter several were suffering from scurvy. All but six of the fifty dogs had died from a mysterious illness. That meant the men themselves would have to manhaul the sledges when they struck north toward the fabled Open Polar Sea.

In February Kane began to prepare for the journey. This went against the advice of both Petersen and Ohlsen, who didn't like the idea of crossing the turbulent expanse of mountainous ice, jagged bergs, thick snow drifts, and howling winds so early in the season. And there were other problems: Kane had to turn his cabin into a jail to hold the unruly Blake.

On March 19 he sent Henry Brooks, his first mate, and seven men to establish a shore depot for the polar dash. But Petersen was right – it *was* far too early. The weather was forty below Fahrenheit (–40° C). The snow was as sharp and as dry as sand. The terrain was unbelievably rough. The weather was so bad the men couldn't move their overloaded sledge. And so they turned back, four of the party so frostbitten they couldn't walk.

Petersen, Ohlsen, and a young German scientist, August

Sonntag, left the others behind and pushed on for help. The ship was thirty miles (48 km) away. If their friends were to survive they wouldn't have time to stop for food, drink, or sleep. They made the trip in thirteen hours, arriving delirious and haggard. Ohlsen had to have his toes amputated because of frostbite. The other two were unable to speak.

Kane gathered up seven seamen and set off with the crippled Ohlsen lashed to the sledge. In spite of his amputated toes the carpenter would have to serve as guide because the others were powerless. The sledge was useless in the tangle of broken ice. The party abandoned it and struggled forward on foot. Ohlsen, half fainting, was supported between two men.

At last they found the tent containing the missing men, half expecting the occupants to be dead. They were grateful to discover them just barely alive. After sleeping in two-hour shifts, they strapped the invalids to their sledge and the party set off for the ship.

This was a nightmare journey. Again and again they were forced to unload the sledge and lift it over a barrier, while the sick lay groaning on the ice. After ten miles (16 km) even the healthy men began dropping in their tracks. Kane and Godfrey raised a tent to cover them up. Then Kane headed out for another nine miles (14.4 km) to pick up the abandoned sledge which they had left behind on the outward journey. Godfrey offered to go with him. Although he was a problem, Kane accepted because he was tougher than the others.

Before they reached their goal, Kane was delirious – babbling and swooning. But Godfrey pushed him along. At one point, Kane thought Godfrey was a bear and called on his imaginary crew to shoot him. By this time his beard was so solidly frozen to his clothing that when they reached the missing sledge Godfrey had to hack off part of it with a jack-knife.

Finally the others caught up. They moved forward at the rate of about a mile and a half (2.4 km) an hour, all demented, seized by a kind of frenzy, laughing frantically, groaning and screaming – a company of madmen.

The safety of the ship was in the hands of the young ship's doctor, Isaac Hayes. He was only twenty-one – a green medical student just out of school. When the half-crazed men reached the ship they looked like corpses, covered from head to foot with frost, their beards lumpy with ice, their eyes vacant and wild. They threw themselves on their bunks and passed out.

To Hayes, the ship "presented all the appearances of a mad house." Two men died, but Kane, the long-time invalid, was the last to collapse and the first to recover.

Shortly after this, a seaman spotted eight people on the shore – Inuit from the community of Etah (seventy miles [112 km] away) the most northerly permanent human habitation in the world. They had never before seen white men. They cheerfully sold Kane four dogs to add to the three healthy animals left on the ship.

When Kane recovered he planned another expedition.

Far to the north lay the great Humboldt Glacier – the most massive ice sheet in the known world. Kane was anxious to visit it. On April 25, he sent a party of six ahead with some of the dogs and followed on after with Godfrey as his sole companion. Even though Godfrey was a problem he had saved Kane's life and was the fittest man and the best dog driver on the ship.

The scenery was spectacular. Red sandstone cliffs, cut by bays and fissures, rose a thousand feet (300 m) from the frozen sea. Ahead, the great glacier sprawled across Greenland, its glittering face looking down on them from a height of four hundred feet (122 m). But they couldn't climb it. Three men had gone blind, another suffered chest pains, several were crippled by scurvy. On May 4, Kane himself almost fainted and with one foot frozen was strapped into the sledge. When he reached the ship ten days later he was in a stupor.

He had failed again. With two of his crew dead and most of the rest shattered, he only had three men healthy enough for duty. Four of the officers were "knocked up," in his phrase. Almost a year had gone by and he had little to show for it. He hadn't found Franklin and, indeed, he hadn't made much effort to find him. He'd seen no evidence of the Open Polar Sea.

Could Franklin have survived? he asked himself. It occurred to him the Inuit might be caring for the lost expedition. He knew that the hundred-mile (160 km) blank spot on his crude map of the Kane Basin must be filled in if

Morton climbs the treacherous cliff of Cape Constitution.

he was to salvage anything from his ill-fated adventure. He sent William Morton, his steward, and Hans Hendrik, the Greenland native, to sledge north to the very top of the basin. This time he knew they *must* succeed.

They staggered back on July 10, their dogs limping, one animal in such bad shape he had to be carried. But they had sensational news. They had found a new channel thirty miles (48 km) wide leading north out of the basin. They had followed it until they had reached a massive cliff – Cape Constitution – jutting into the water. At that point they had gone eighty miles (128 km) farther north than any other white explorer.

Morton, clawing his way for five hundred feet (152 m) up the rocky precipice, had seen a marvellous spectacle – open water as far as the eye could view. The cliffs were a-flutter with sea fowl; the glittering sea was free of ice. Kane was certain that what Morton had seen was the Open Polar Sea.

Of course he was wrong. The magical waters Morton saw in the distance were simply the product of wind, waves, and wishful thinking.

Such mirages are common in the Arctic, as they are in the desert, and for similar reasons. They are caused when the air close to the ground is denser than the air above. Sailors often saw distant ships upside down, as in a spyglass, and apparently floating in the sky – or even ranges of non-existent mountains on the horizon.

Kane, however, believed Morton's discovery more than

justified the horrors he had been through. "I can say that I have led an expedition whose results will be remembered for all time," he wrote.

Food and fuel were growing scarce and it was obvious that the officers and crew were unreliable. Kane knew he must try again to justify the expedition – especially to his family who viewed it with such foreboding. "I hope, if I have the health to fill up my notes that I may advance myself in my father's eyes by a book on glaciers and glacial geology," he wrote. But he was faced with the dreadful possibility of a second winter in the Arctic.

By August, except for a little hot coffee and soup, the men were existing on cold salt pork. Then they found they could not blast their ship out of the frozen ice of the harbour. Kane realized the worst: "It is *horrible* – yes, that is the word – to look forward to another year of disease and darkness to be met without fresh food and without fuel."

Was he also to suffer the fate of Franklin? The winter was closing in. He left an account of his discoveries in a cairn, encased in glass and sealed up with melted lead. On the nearby cliff in huge letters he painted the name of his ship. The coffins of the two dead crew members lay buried beneath. How many more graves would there be before the winter was over?

CHAPTER FOUR

~

"The most perfect hellhole"

KANE'S DEALINGS WITH HIS crew – especially the officers – grew worse. The men were insolent, refusing to attend evening prayers. In fact, the crew despised their captain. John Wilson, Kane's sailing master, claimed that Kane couldn't walk through the ship "without hearing his name used in the most insolent manner by the men in the forecastle." As for the officers, he wrote, "there wasn't one who would trust one word he said or place a particle of confidence in him. He does nothing but quarrel from morning to night with those around him." When the captain wasn't quarrelling he was boasting – about his narrow escapes, his global adventures, his reception by foreign heads of state, and the costly dinners at which he had been the host.

We must remember that discontent of this kind was common among seamen cooped up for twelve months or more on a tiny, uncomfortable wooden ship in a strange and hostile land. The history of Arctic exploration is full of such problems. But there is no doubt that Kane was a difficult captain and one who had little experience in handling men.

The constant arguments were too much for Christian Ohlsen, the carpenter who Kane had appointed to replace Henry Brooks as first mate. Ohlsen quit that job in June. Kane soon became aware of secret meetings in Ohlsen's quarters and also in Isaac Hayes's. Men would gather in groups whispering together. Finally, Morton came to report that several wanted to leave the ship rather than spend another winter in the Arctic. Their plan was to make their way to Upernavik, the northernmost of the Greenland settlements, seven hundred miles (1,120 km) to the south.

To Kane these men were traitors. Yet he knew that if he refused them permission to leave, there would be even worse problems. On August 24, he called his company together to warn them of the dangers they faced and gave them twenty-four hours to make up their minds.

He got his answer the following day. All but five men agreed to leave. Of the loyalists, only Morton and "Irish Tom" Hickey, the cabin boy, were fit for duty. The others were too ill to work.

To Kane's dismay, four of his officers were determined to leave. He could understand Hayes: he was a doctor and the party would need him. But he felt the other officers' decisions were close to treachery. Finally two men, Wilson and James McGary, agreed to stay.

Now nine of the ship's company were preparing to

leave. Kane wouldn't even talk to them. He agreed to give them some food and equipment and a boat, which Ohlsen would build. He advised them to elect a leader and they chose Ohlsen.

Ohlsen couldn't make up his mind. Kane now insisted that he and the others sign a statement that from the moment they left the ship they would be under their own control and their connection with the expedition would be regarded as closed. When Ohlsen refused, Kane withdrew his permission for Ohlsen to leave, warning that he would shoot him as a deserter. Ohlsen had no choice but to remain.

The others took three days to get organized. The good-byes were remarkably friendly. Kane even broke out his private stock of champagne. Inwardly he seethed with a black rage. He saw them as deserters who had betrayed him by leaving their posts and he washed his hands of them.

The captain saw himself as a martyr victimized by traitors. "I have made up my mind to act towards these miserable men without a thought of self ... God will take care of us. I did not know before this awful prospect of a second winter that I had so much faith," he wrote.

The departing crew members quarrelled among themselves. Actually, they became panic-stricken when their small sledge went through the ice and almost drowned them. One man, George Riley, went back to the ship. But the seven remaining deserters vanished into the mists of the south. On September 5, 1854, all connections were cut.

Kane was outwardly calm. But into his journal he poured out all his feelings of betrayal, his sense of personal injury, and his self-justification of the events of the previous weeks.

"… They are deserters, in act and in spirit – in all but the title. They leave their ship, abandon their sick comrades, fail to adhere to their commander, and are false to the implied trust which tells every true man to abide by the

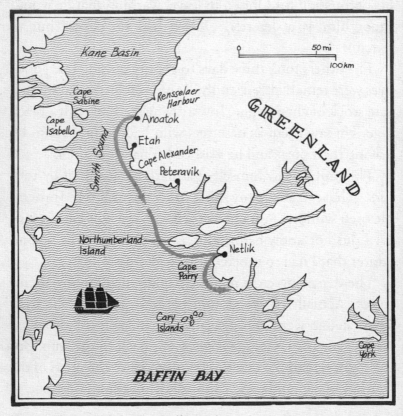

Route of Kane's defectors, Fall 1854

Expedition into which he has entered…. this misguided party have wanted for nothing – they have had the best of everything, even at self sacrifice…. They should have had the same treatment had they spit in my face."

He was certain they would come back, many of them broken down, to seek a refuge on board. He would give it to them but he would never trust them again. In his mind they were "low minded sneaks."

Now Kane had to protect the ship for the winter. He turned part of it into a reasonable copy of an Inuit igloo. The crew tore the planking off the upper deck to use as firewood. They sealed the quarterdeck with a padding of moss and turf. Then they built a living space just eighteen feet (5.5 m) square, lining the ceiling and floors with moss and caulking the floor with oakum and plaster of Paris. To reach these cramped quarters the crew would have to crawl through a long, narrow passage between the decks. This would be their home for the next eight or ten months.

Kane also knew he would have to depend on the Inuit for fresh seal and walrus meat to stave off scurvy, and also for dogs to haul sledges. But he discovered, to his dismay, that a band of natives with whom he had been dealing had made off with his cooking utensils and buffalo robes. He knew he'd have to stop any further pilfering.

He sent his two best hikers, Morton and Riley, to the tiny community of Anoatok, halfway between the ship and the main Inuit village of Etah. There they found three of the culprits – a boy and two women asleep with their loot.

They took drastic steps. They sent the boy to Etah to report to the headman, Metek, and then kidnapped the two women. One of these was Metek's wife. She would be used as bait to bring the headman back to the brig with a sledload of the stolen goods.

With that done, Kane made a formal treaty with the Inuit. They promised to supply him with fresh meat and dogs and to stop stealing. On his part he swore to give them presents and guns with which to hunt.

There was a worse problem. A body of rats had left the ship's hold for the warmth of Kane's makeshift igloo. There were rats everywhere – under the stove, in the cushions, in the lockers, in the bedding. They chewed away at furs, woollens, shoes, specimens – everything. When Kane put his hand into his mitten one day he was bitten by a mother rat that was raising her brood inside. And before he could stop the blood the rat family ran off with the mitten!

Kane put the rats to good use. After all, he'd been all over the world eating everything from bats to puppy dogs. He had already become used to eating raw blubber with the Inuit, and so now he simply cooked and ate the rats. Many of the company suffered from scurvy but Kane didn't, thanks to the fresh meat.

As the weeks dragged by, the ship was slowly stripped of all firewood. The upper deck, bulwark, fancy shelving, and bulkheads were gone by early November. The crew's morale was shattered. One man, McGary, became so homesick he refused to eat anything.

Kane confessed to moments of despair: "My thoughts,

my diseased craving for love and caressment, everything that unbends, I crush, strangle, before they take shape. The Father – I cease to remember his years – the Mother – I will not count her tears – weeping on her wet pillow for her first-born and her last."

But as captain he couldn't allow these feelings to show. In fact he continued his dictatorial style, which added to the tensions. Kane took out his inner rage on the youngest member of the crew, Tom Hickey. But nobody really escaped his outbursts.

To Wilson, the cramped cabin was "the most perfect hellhole." About Kane, he wrote: "From the time he gets up in the morning till we are all turned in he is incessantly quarrelling with someone or making use of his arbitrary power." Kane never went to bed until three or four in the morning and never rose until after noon. And that caused problems, for he made everybody else get up early.

He saw himself through different eyes, as a stern parent keeping his difficult children in line. "… If the Lord does not blot me out and I will return as a man who has braved a hard temptation and abided by his trust, then those who live either with me, or after me … will give me credit for something more than a blind will & a groping material-ism…."

Kane was lonely. He was cut off from the one man with whom he might have been friends. This was Henry Good-fellow, whom Kane had taken on as a natural history observer as a favour to Kane's brother, Tom. Goodfellow was worse than useless. Wilson found him "lazy, dirty, ragged and impudent to everyone." Kane thought him "one of the most impractical and helpless men I was ever connected with."

As the days went by, Goodfellow neglected his duty, refused to look after himself, and withdrew from his shipmates, most of whom wouldn't speak to him. Finally Kane took over Goodfellow's duties himself and while the others toiled, Goodfellow lounged about, reading novels.

Though Kane could never speak to him "without disgust," he still catered to him. He had looked upon

Desperate crew members tear apart the Advance *for firewood.*

Goodfellow as his closest friend, a man of his own social class. Now he was doing his jobs for him, even carrying glasses of lime juice and water when asked. "He has more cool impudence than any man I ever knew," Kane wrote of his former friend.

By early December, five of the crew were sick with scurvy. The only medicine available was the gratings from raw potatoes. Scurvy comes about from a lack of fresh vegetables and fruits. There were only old potatoes left and these were three years old at least. But that was all they had.

The three healthy men were put to work tearing the oak ribbing off the ship for firewood. Kane managed to collect a ton (907 kg) of fuel this way. He knew it wouldn't last past January. For February and March he counted on using three inches (7.6 cm) of oak sheathing nailed to the ship's side as protection against ice. That would give them two and a half more tons (2,236 kg) of firewood.

At three o'clock in the morning of December 7, Kane was awakened with the news that five sledges with six teams of dogs, each with strange drivers, were approaching the ship. A few minutes later, a group of Inuit came aboard supporting his former shipmates, Bonsall and Petersen, both of whom were in dreadful condition. They had left the brig fourteen weeks before, but as Kane had prophesied they hadn't been able to get to Upernavik. They reported that the others, exhausted and starving, were crouched in a stone hovel some hundred and fifty miles (240 km) to the south. The pair had managed to get back to the brig by bribing the southern Inuit. Now they pleaded for help for their comrades.

Kane acted at once, gathered up a hundred pounds of provisions, and sent them off with the strange natives. Petersen and Bonsall were so sick they couldn't move. Kane and the able-bodied men couldn't desert the sick aboard the ship. He didn't trust the new natives to take the food back to the others, but he had no choice. He gave them presents, sent them on their way, and hoped for the best.

Chapter Five

~

Saved by the Inuit

W HAT HAD HAPPENED TO the "deserters" who had left for the south the previous August? The eight men were an odd lot – a German astronomer, a Baltimore seaman, a Pennsylvania farmer, a Greenland cooper, a Hull sailor, an East River boatman, an Irish patriot, and a Philadelphia medical student.

Only the Greenlander, Petersen, had any Arctic experience, but he was not the one who was really in charge. The man on whom they depended for life or death was a cheerful and talkative Inuit medicine man from the village of Netlik. His name was Kalutunah. Kane and his crew met him the first winter. Now the deserters ran into him again as they struggled slowly in their two small boats through the tangled wilderness of ice. By the time they reached Netlik on the coast near Northumberland Island, they were running short of food and fuel. Kalutunah's people gave them blubber to eat and moss for lamp wicks in return for needles and knives.

Four days later, on September 16, the ice closed in for good. Now they knew they had no hope of getting to civilization before spring. They went to work in the bitter cold, trying to build a shelter on the shore using huge stones chinked with moss, and some tin and lumber taken from the two boats.

Finally, on October 9, they moved into what Dr. Hayes called, "a cold, fireless, damp, vault-like den." By October 18 they had eaten all their biscuits and now had to survive on rock moss which produced dreadful stomach cramps. Certain death faced them.

Then, two days later, they were saved when two strange-looking creatures, covered from head to foot in a coating of ice and snow, crawled into the hut. This was Kalutunah and a companion. They'd travelled for thirty-six hours without stopping to bring frozen meat and blubber. The men fell on it like wolves.

Clearly they couldn't survive without help from the natives, who were eager for white men's goods. Petersen was the only one who spoke their language. He arranged a treaty in which the white men would be supplied with food in exchange for knives, needles, and other treasures. But Kalutunah wouldn't rent them any dogs or sledges. Obviously, he didn't want them to get away.

After supplying the party with enough meat for one meal and some blubber for fuel, the two Inuit left. It was two weeks before they returned. In the meantime the men, who didn't know enough to hunt, survived on rock moss, growing steadily weaker. They recovered when the Inuit came back with several days' supply of blubber.

It was maddening. The Inuit gave them only enough food or fuel to keep them alive. Here they were – eight men from the civilized world – trapped in a tiny shack, unable to bring in more than an occasional fox or ptarmigan in spite of their superior weapons. Yet the Inuit came and went at will, apparently unaffected by the weather. One day a young woman turned up with a six-month-old baby strapped to her back. She had travelled forty miles (64 km) – in minus thirty-five degree Fahrenheit (–37° C) weather – often getting off the dogsled and walking. The only reason for her trip was to see the white strangers.

They knew they had to get away. Their only chance was to send back to the ship for more supplies, and try to reach the whaling fleet in the spring. Petersen agreed to go to the village with Kalutunah and bargain for dogs and sleds. Godfrey offered to go with him.

The two men reached the village on November 3. At first they were well fed and well treated. But as time passed, Petersen, a cautious Dane who had lived among the Inuit for twenty years and was married to one, began to feel uneasy. Many strangers began to crowd into the village including a glowering dog driver named Sip-su, who boasted that he'd killed two members of his own tribe because they couldn't hunt. And Kalutunah seemed to be under Sip-su's spell.

Petersen was anxious to be on his way, but now nobody volunteered to go with him. He quietly warned Godfrey in the next hut to be on his guard and told the natives that if anything happened to him his friends would arrive with their magic guns and kill them all.

His only security lay in the Inuit's belief that he had a pistol. The natives were convinced it was a magic wand, for they had never seen a gun. It was this fear that saved him. Actually he had no pistol, and the rifle, which the natives feared, lay outside the hut.

Pretending to sleep, Petersen heard Sip-su telling the others that he would lead an attack on the white men with Kalutunah as his lieutenant. Petersen opened his eyes just as Sip-su started to search his clothing for the non-existent pistol. Outside the hut a crowd had gathered around Petersen's rifle, afraid to touch it. Petersen seized it and announced he was going off to hunt for bear.

He alerted Godfrey and the two set off immediately on a forty-mile (64 km) trek back to Hayes and the others. They had gone no more than two miles (3.2 km) before the natives gave chase. Petersen brandished the magic rifle and that kept them at a distance.

But the pair could not sleep. If the natives didn't get them, the cold would. Drowsy, exhausted, starving and mad with thirst, they reached their goal after trudging for twenty-four hours. "Water! Water!" they cried as they stumbled into the hut. They had survived only because they had been fed well during the previous three days.

The party of seamen prepared for an attack. Instead, Kalutunah appeared, all smiles, and brought them a large piece of walrus meat. Hayes was convinced that the Inuit had been influenced by a bad leader and he was right. It turned out that Kalutunah had opposed Sip-su's ideas. Fortunately for everybody, Sip-su's courage had failed him in the presence of the magic gun.

Now the party managed to get five dogs from the natives. But it was not possible to get back to the brig. After a few miles the attempt failed, and they returned, stupefied by cold. The following morning the two strongest men, Petersen and Bonsall, set off by themselves for Kane's ship. Those left behind again had no food except for pieces of walrus hide, and by the third day even that was gone.

The desperate men believed now that the Inuit intended to leave them to their fate. The natives wouldn't take the party north, or rent them dog teams. It seemed they were determined to let the men starve to death before plundering the hut. But Hayes had no intention of allowing that. He didn't want to murder the Inuit. But his plan was to put them to sleep with laudanum, a form of opium. Then they would steal the Inuit dogs and sleds and head for the ship.

He made a soup of the two pieces of meat that the Inuit allowed them. He slipped the contents of a vial of the laudanum into their soup bowls. Then while the whites watched, the natives ate greedily and soon became drowsy. Hayes and the others helped them off with their coats and boots and then moved quickly to put on their own travelling clothes.

They knew they had no time to lose. They crawled out of the hut taking the natives' boots, mittens, and coats with them. Then they barricaded the doorway as best they could.

The journey that followed was clumsy. No one understood how to handle Inuit dogs. One sledge overturned and the dogs squirmed out of their traces and fled back to the hut. With three men on each of the remaining two sledges the party blundered on as far as Cape Parry where they found shelter in a cave.

Their freedom was short-lived. The Inuit had awoken quickly and, with their usual ingenuity, made mukluks out of blankets, cut up other blankets as ponchos, found the lost sled and the wandering dogs, and quickly picked up the party's trail.

Since they knew how to handle the dogs, it was no trick to catch up with the white men. There they stood, silent accusers, their heads sticking out of the blankets – one red, one white, one blue – their feet wrapped in old cloths and, in one case, a discarded pair of boots, and their arms filled with the treasure they could not bear to abandon – tin cups, saucers, cutlery, even an old hat. The situation would have been ludicrous had it not been so threatening.

Hayes held them off with a rifle. The Inuit pleaded with them not to shoot. Hayes took two prisoners, and in sign language offered a deal. If Kalutunah would drive the party north, they would return the dogs, sledges, and clothes. Otherwise, they would shoot them all. Kalutunah cheerfully agreed.

Now they moved north through a series of small Inuit

settlements. The Inuit there treated them well. Finally, they reached the larger village of Etah, but not without a terrifying journey around Cape Alexander, where they were forced to cling to a narrow shelf on the cliffside, no more than fifteen inches (38 cm) wide, high above the sea.

When they reached Etah they discovered that Petersen's Inuit had eaten all the food that Kane had sent back. They still had seventy miles (112 km) to go! By the time they reached the brig one man was stupefied by cold, the others were at a breaking point.

"We come here destitute and exhausted to claim your hospitality," Hayes said. "We know we have no rights to your indulgence, but we feel that with you we will have a welcome and a home."

Kane took one look at him – covered with snow, fainting from hunger – grasped his hand and beckoned his companions aboard. The young doctor's feet were so badly frostbitten that Kane had to amputate several of his toes. He gave Hayes his own bed to sleep in.

But he did not forgive him.

CHAPTER SIX

Retreat

KANE FORGAVE NO ONE. He now had eight more men on his crowded ship than he had planned for. They had no food or equipment, and only the clothes on their backs – not even blankets. They had lost everything they had taken with them. He had expected to last out the winter with a small, but faithful company and then make a dash for the sea. Now he had almost double the number he had reckoned on.

The loyal party that had stayed with Kane was bitter at the returnees.

"God in Heaven," the explorer wrote in his private journal, "it makes my blood boil!" He took out his anger with his pencil, in page after page, railing against the men who had defected. "These men can never be my associates again," he wrote.

And so, in that cramped little vessel with its one crowded room, he ordered a strange arrangement. He would divide the ship's company into two groups – the faithful and the unfaithful. Each would eat separately. The unfaithful wouldn't be allowed to do any work on the ship. They could contribute to their own routine, but would be treated merely as guests. The faithful would do all the work, but since most were down with scurvy, or useless, that meant that Kane himself must take on most of the burden.

There was another problem. The two malcontents, Blake and Godfrey, were so unpopular they had to eat by themselves. That caused a battle in which Kane bashed in Blake's skull with a belaying pin and knocked Godfrey to the ground. Blake suffered a concussion but recovered. Kane told him if he disobeyed again he would kill him.

As the winter wore on, tempers continued to fray. Wilson was convinced Kane's brain had become unhinged. Fresh meat was scarce. Even Hans, the Inuit hunter, couldn't find much. And at Etah, the Inuit too were starving.

Although the crew still remained divided between the faithful and the unfaithful, to use Kane's terms, he had to call upon the healthier of the former deserters to help with the work. By March, fourteen men were flat on their backs with scurvy.

He faced a more serious problem. Godfrey and Blake were planning to steal dogs, a sledge, and provisions, and leave for the south.

Kane rose on the morning of March 20, armed himself, and ordered Godfrey to cook breakfast. Then he crawled through the narrow passageway between decks that led to the sleeping quarters and waited. Blake appeared first and then Godfrey. Kane leaped out and thrust a pistol an inch from Godfrey's nose. When Godfrey confessed to a plot, Kane knocked him down and hammered him with a piece of lead concealed inside his mitt. But he faced a real problem. He couldn't jail either man because he needed them to help. As a result, Godfrey managed to slip away. When Kane sent Hans south with sledges to get meat at Etah, Godfrey caught up with him and took his team.

Hans didn't come back. Only a few ptarmigan shot by Petersen kept the invalids alive. Then, on April 2, a man was seen a mile from the brig. Was it Hans? No – it was William Godfrey with two dogs and a sled-load of walrus meat. He had made a seventy mile (112 km) trip on foot in fifty below (−46° C) weather to reach Etah in just thirty hours – something no one else had been able to do. He reported that Hans was ill and that he, himself, had decided to live with the Inuit. Kane threatened to shoot him but his rifle wouldn't fire in the cold. Godfrey walked away just as a bullet whistled over his head. He made it back to Etah.

The meat that he'd brought was a godsend. Kane was suspicious of both the absent Godfrey and his crony, Blake, who was still aboard ship. He was convinced they were planning some mischief. He needed to put up a show of discipline; otherwise others might follow Godfrey's example. He called his men together and warned that anyone who deserted would be shot.

He couldn't let Godfrey get away with it, and so on April 10 set off for Etah by himself. There he found Hans hunting seal. He wasn't ill any more but he was in love with a young Inuit woman named Merkut who had nursed him when he was sick. Kane got Hans back to the brig and then again turned his attention to Godfrey.

Kane now disguised himself as an Inuit, took one of Hans' friends with him, armed himself with a six-shooter, packed a set of leg irons, found Godfrey in a hut at Etah, and forced him back at gunpoint.

Hans would not stay on the ship. He set off to Etah, apparently to get some walrus hide to make some boots. Actually, he wanted to return to Merkut, and this was the last Kane saw of him. The two were married and went off to raise a family, and that was that.

Now Kane knew that he would have to abandon the ship. She was a sorry-looking sight that May – her upper spars, bulwarks, deck sheathing, stanchions, bulkheads, hatches, ice timbers, and railings had all been torn away for fuel. Every bit of rope, everything burnable down to the last broomstick, had been sacrificed to keep the crew from freezing to death.

They would have to make their way south to Upernavik by small boat.

Kane got the healthier men building runners to haul two large boats and a smaller dinghy over the snows to reach open water. That lay eighty miles (128 km) to the south at Naviliak, on the coast not far from Etah.

They faced a terrible ordeal: everything – three boats, fifteen hundred pounds (684 kg) of supplies, and four invalids – would have to be shuttled a mile or so between rests, by men already weakened by scurvy and hunger. The sick

Crew members build sledge runners for the trek to Upernavik.

were placed in a halfway house in Anoatok. It took the others thirty-one days to move everything to the open sea. In that time – May 17 to June 18 – the exhausted men, so weak they could only pull one boat at a time, each trudged a distance of three hundred and sixteen miles (506 km).

Kane did more than that. He travelled constantly by dogsled – to Etah to get food, to Anoatok to look after the invalids, then back to the brig to help bake bread. Altogether this remarkable man covered 1,100 miles (1,760 km). Then, on the final lap, Christian Ohlsen came to grief. One of the runners of his boat had broken through the surface and only his strength kept it from swamping, while the others pulled it back to solid ice. But Ohlsen had ruptured his bladder and a few days later he died.

Kane later acknowledged that without the Inuit they would never have made it. The entire population of Etah turned out to wave them goodbye as the two whaleboats, *Faith* and *Hope,* set off on June 19. For the next forty-nine days they fought their way through blizzards, pack ice, and bergs.

Kane insisted that every man get his rest at night, even though it meant lying under ice-sheathed cliffs in their buffalo robes, or sleeping aboard the boats. To keep up the crew's morale, the captain continued morning and evening prayers. No longer idle, the company knew now their only hope of survival lay in working as a team.

Soon their food was almost exhausted. Kane allowed each of his crew only six ounces (170 g) of bread dust a day, plus a walnut-sized lump of tallow. The men were losing their muscular power as they dragged their boats through veins of water between the ice fields. Kane knew they would have to find food quickly or die.

The flotilla tied up to a great ice floe, from whose peak he could see in the distance the red face of Cape Dalrymple Rock. At that very point a gale hit the flotilla. The ice floe was hurled and crushed against the base of the rock and the men were helplessly whirled about in their boats. Using boat hooks they forced themselves into a stretch of open water. When the tide rose they pulled their craft over an ice shelf and into a gorge where, too weak to unload their supplies, they dropped in their tracks and slept.

Fortunately there was food. They gathered ducks' eggs – twelve hundred in a single day – and shot sea fowl. To keep them going on the next leg of their voyage they now had two hundred pounds of dried meat.

At Cape Dudley Diggs, the tongue of a great glacier barred their way. Kane, climbing a berg, saw to his dismay that here the season was late. The ice still blocked their way; they would have to wait for the delayed summer to open a lane. He could not bear to tell the others. They waited another week, crept forward in their battered craft to Cape York, and waited again.

It was July 21. There was game but no fuel. To cook the meat, they were forced to burn oars, sledge runners, and finally the little dinghy, *Red Eric*. They set off again and found, after an exhausting journey, that they had mistakenly entered a false inlet that led nowhere. The prospect of repairing the sledges and retracing their steps with the boats again on runners was so horrifying that even McGary, the toughest of the crew, was reduced to tears. It took three days of backbreaking toil.

By the time they crossed Melville Bay their food was gone. Only the lucky capture of a seal saved them from starving to death. Then at last, on August 1, they sighted the famous landmark known as the Devil's Thumb, a huge bulbous peak that told them they'd entered the whaling grounds of Baffin Bay.

Two days later, Petersen came upon the first native they'd seen since leaving Etah. To his joy, he recognized an old friend, paddling his kayak on the search for eider among the islands.

"Paul Zacharias," Petersen cried. "Don't you know me? I'm Carl Petersen."

The man stared at him in fright. "No," he said, "his wife says he's dead," and he paddled off as fast as he could.

Another two days, and a new sound was heard as the men rowed along. It wasn't the gulls; it wasn't the cry of a fox; it was the soft slapping of oars accompanied by a low "halloo!"

"What is it!" Kane asked.

Petersen listened for a moment and then in a trembling half-whisper exclaimed: "*Dannemarkers!*"

The cry echoed again from a nearby cape, then died. Both boats pulled toward it, scanning the shore. Had it all been a dream?

Half an hour passed. Then the single mast of a small

shallop showed itself. Petersen began to sob and to cry out, half in English, half in Danish. It was, he said, an Upernavik oil boat. He knew it well: The *Fraulein Flairscher.* "Carlie Mossyn the assistant cooper must be on his road to Kingatok for blubber!"

Petersen was right; in a moment Carlie Mossyn himself appeared. Kane's crew was hungry for news of the outside world, which they had left two years before, and pleaded with Petersen to translate their questions.

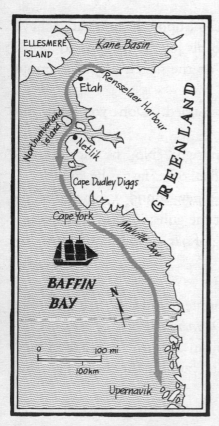

"What of America? Eh, Petersen?"

"We don't know much of that country here, for they have no whalers on the coast," said Carlie, "but a steamer and a barque passed up a fortnight ago, and have gone out into the ice to seek your party."

And then he added, as if an afterthought, "Sebastopol ain't taken." That was gibberish to the men, who hadn't heard of the Crimean War between Great Britain and Russia

Kane's retreat, Spring 1855

(1854-56), and the battle to capture that city on the Black Sea.

Now they learned for the first time that the first clues to Franklin's fate – bones of his crew members – had been found a thousand miles (1,600 km) to the southwest. At last Kane realized his searches had been for nothing. Still, he could take heart in his discoveries, for he had moved his ship farther north in the western Arctic than any other white man. He had explored much of the basin that today bears his name. He discovered the largest glacier in the known world. He thought he had "proved" the existence of an Open Polar Sea.

More important, however, was the fact that, through an exercise of willpower, careful planning, and discipline, he had managed on this trek from the ship to bring all but one of his bickering crew through some of the most difficult waters in the world to a safe haven in a friendly Greenland port.

The following night, August 6, 1855, he and his men slept under a civilized roof for the time since leaving the *Advance*. But after eighty-four days in the open air they did not sleep well, for they were no longer used to civilization.

CHAPTER SEVEN

~
A national hero

ELISHA KANE RETURNED TO America in the fall of 1855 to find himself a popular hero. The journal he had written during the first expedition, with its haunting descriptions of icebergs and its terrifying account of being trapped in Wellington Channel, had been published when he was away. Congress had voted one hundred and fifty thousand dollars to send two ships to search for him.

Luckily, Kane was found at Godhavn after the two search ships, blocked by the ice on Smith Sound, returned to southern Greenland. His younger brother John had accompanied the rescue expedition but didn't recognize the gaunt, bearded creature in the strange, wild costume.

However, by the time the two expeditions reached New York in October, with cannons roaring and crowds cheering, Kane was looking healthier than he had when he left more than two years before. His body had fleshed out, his face was bronze, his neatly-trimmed black beard showed only a touch of grey.

He went straight to the home of his sponsor, Henry Grinnell.

"I have no *Advance* with me," were his first words.

"Never mind," Grinnell told him. "You are safe; that is all we care about. Come into the parlour and tell us the whole story." But Kane never did tell the whole story. His bitterness over what he considered the traitorous actions of his crew, his battles with Godfrey and Blake, his exasperation with Goodfellow and the others, were either left out or toned down in the accounts that followed.

Yet there was still enough on the day after his arrival for the *New York Times* to devote its entire front page to his adventure. The book, on which he worked that winter – his second – sold sixty-five thousand copies, made him a small fortune, and turned him into a national hero.

Although they were based on his own journals, they gave a different picture of the man than the fevered narrative scrawled out in his own hand during the long Arctic nights. The Kane of the best-sellers is a much softer, kindlier man than the Kane revealed in the pages of the journals.

His reputation as a brilliant leader and bold explorer rests almost entirely on the two books. The public and the press of course, never saw his personal journal, or that of his sailing master, John Wall Wilson. They had no insight into his flawed leadership, his unruly temperament, his quirky personality, or his towering ego. Wilson tried to write a book of his own but Kane paid him $350 to suppress it.

Kane's best-seller didn't appeal to some of his former shipmates, especially Hayes and Bonsall. They felt he had taken too much of the glory himself. Godfrey wrote an account of his own, but it received little attention. Kane's literary style laid the foundation for his reputation as "the outstanding polar idol of the mid-century."

In truth, he was a better writer than explorer. That is his real contribution to the history of Arctic discovery. It was his graphic tale, prominently displayed on the bookshelves of the nation, that caught the imagination of others and caused them to continue the polar quest.

He was indeed as popular as any modern astronaut, sports hero or rock star – more popular perhaps, for in those days any man who risked his life in an unknown corner of

Margaret Fox watches the crowds cheer Kane's triumphal arrival in New York.

the world was worshipped far above the common herd. Without films, television, or radio, people depended upon the written word; and here Kane had few equals.

It's important to remember that without Kalutunah and his Inuit comrades, Kane's second voyage would have been a disaster. Indeed, it is doubtful if any of that odd company would have survived without the help of the natives.

Kane himself adopted many of the native methods. The igloo he created aboard his ship to survive the winter was certainly based on their own dwellings. Had Franklin and

his dying crew paid more attention to Inuit life and practices, it's possible they too might have survived. But the British refused to adopt the Arctic way of life.

Back in New York, there was Kane's romance with Margaret Fox – an object of great interest in the press. She was not in Pennsylvania, where he had sent her. She was back in New York, living with a friend. As soon as he landed in New York, she waited breathlessly for him to call. But she waited in vain.

Margaret could hear the guns heralding the arrival of her lost love. Alas for her, the night passed with no word from him. The following day Henry Grinnell's son, Cornelius, who had been placed in charge of her, arrived to explain that the explorer was ill with rheumatism. He was also concerned about his family and friends who did not approve of the match with Margaret. Cornelius told her that Kane would come when he was able to. This didn't sound like the same ardent adventurer who had poured out his love to her in a series of letters before vanishing into the Arctic's mists.

In fact, Kane had not mentioned her in his private journal and certainly not in any of his public works. He was a man who had always blown hot and cold, and if he was having second thoughts about Margaret that is not surprising. His family had always exerted a powerful influence upon him and was now in such a state of alarm they tried to get back the letters he wrote to her.

Kane was torn between his love and respect for his parents and his attachment to Margaret. Forty-eight hours went by after his triumphal arrival. Finally he came to her and an up-and-down relationship continued all winter.

On that first visit she was so overcome she wouldn't see him at first. Then she was in his arms as he showered her with kisses. To her dismay, he told her that any thought of marriage would have to be postponed because of his family's opposition. He said they would be as brother and sister – nothing more. He even forced her to sign a document making such a promise. She did so in tears. Later he sent it back and she tore it up.

Kane had never approved of the séances. He was afraid that Margaret would go back to becoming a spirit rapper. On the other hand, her mother and her sister, Leah, wanted her to return to the stage. She had, after all, been their main source of income.

Both families appeared to be against this marriage. At that, Kane rebelled. He told Margaret his love was stronger than ever. But there is little evidence of that. He himself was dependent on his own family for support until his book was finished. For Margaret that was the end. "I've seen you for the last time," she wrote. "I have been deceived."

At that Kane rushed to her side. He told her that he had betrayed her. "The world shall not say that you, Maggie, are the discarded one!" he cried. "No! – it is you who reject me – Dr. Kane is the discarded lover!" And with that, he threw himself on his knees, pleading, "Speak, Maggie! my destiny is in your hands!"

At least that is the way she described it. For we only have

her own account of these events. However, there was undoubtedly some truth in the story. The press was now asking questions, publishing rumours and details, guessing at the possibility of a broken engagement. And so during Kane's trip to New York, they continued to see each other. Then in February, Mrs. Fox forbade him to visit or write to her again. That had little effect.

Meanwhile, he was working furiously on his book. By May, 1856, the two-volume work was almost complete. It would run to nine hundred pages. Kane received the coveted gold medal of the Geographical Society of Great Britain.

At about this time, Lady Franklin, who was still stubbornly keeping up her crusade to find her missing husband, appealed to Kane to help in the search. She wanted him to take command of a ship to search for relics of her husband's lost expedition which had been found on King William Island. By this time, however, Kane was too ill to return north.

Lady Franklin would not be put off. She needed him. If he couldn't command a ship, at least he could help her with the campaign to persuade the British to send another expedition to search for the lost men. Kane was tempted. He was certain he could convince the British admiralty to support the cause. He was also certain that if he totally withdrew from the project it would collapse. Lady Franklin told him she would cross the Atlantic to persuade him, but that wasn't necessary. He decided to go to her.

Undoubtedly he was also tempted by the prospect of the welcome he would receive in Europe. He was an international figure. He knew he would be a great celebrity on the far side of the Atlantic. His book was about to be published. After a few days in England, basking in the celebrations, he planned to go to Switzerland to restore his health.

He was, in fact, very ill. Grinnell said that "he is but a skeleton, or a shadow of one." He made plans to sail in October with his new valet and servant, the faithful William Morton.

He was still seeing Margaret Fox. He took her to the opera, and to the home of friends in New York. She wrote in her memoirs that there was one final ceremony in which the pair entered into a sort of a marriage. She said that Kane had spent the evening discussing his health and the possibility that he might die. He feared that she might not come to him if he called. He asked if they might not announce their marriage formally in front of witnesses.

He told her, she said, that that would be "sufficient to constitute a legal marriage," and so she agreed. Four persons, including her mother, were there. Kane took her by the hand, and said: "Maggie is my wife, and I am her husband. Wherever we are, she is mine, and I am hers. Do you understand and consent to this, Maggie?"

She agreed, or so she wrote years later. And from that moment she called herself Mrs. Kane. After all, if he died, she would, as his widow, receive a large sum.

He, himself, was concerned about the future: "Maggie,

what if I should die away from you! Oh, my own Maggie, could I but die in your arms, I would ask no more."

It was a wish he could not be granted. He sailed for England on October 11. She never saw him again.

He arrived in London with his heart seriously weakened. He had planned to stay only a few days, then seek a warmer climate. Lady Franklin visited him daily, gave him cod liver oil, brought him books to read. But she continued to act as if he were in command of the search expedition.

He had no intention of taking that on. He was determined to make it clear to her that his determination to withdraw from command a year before was still in force.

A series of dinners, ceremonies, presentations, and other honours kept him longer in England than he had planned. In the end, his doctor persuaded him to visit Cuba where the weather was better. He and Morton left on November 17. Three months later, with his mother and his two brothers at his side, paralyzed by two successive strokes, he died quietly.

The funeral journey that followed was the most spectacular the United States had ever known, exceeded in that century only by that of Abraham Lincoln. It took a month from Havana, Cuba, to New Orleans, up the Mississippi and Ohio to Cincinnati, and then by train to Philadelphia, the levees and wharfs of the great rivers black with people, the stations in Ohio and Pennsylvania crowded with so many mourners that the tracks were jammed and the train held up.

Bands played, dirges droned, guns boomed, bells tolled, and the air was purple with oratory. At every major river port and whistle-stop the casket came off the train and the body of the "Great Explorer, Ripe Scholar, and Noble Philanthropist" lay in state.

In Philadelphia, seven of Kane's old comrades, including Hayes, Bonsall, Goodfellow, and even Godfrey, followed the bier to Independence Hall, where for three days thousands of mourners filed by.

Kane's ceremonial sword lay on the coffin encircled by a garland of flowers. Only one other tribute lay beside it – a splendid wreath with the message "To the Memory of Dr. Kane from Two Ladies." There was no doubt that the two ladies were the Fox sisters. But Kane himself was one with the spirits. And if from the darkness of his tomb – as cold as the Arctic night – he rapped out a message for posterity, there was none to hear him.

Index

Coming Soon

TRAPPED IN THE ARCTIC

Few ideas gripped the minds of Victorian Age explorers more than that of the North West Passage. The belief that there was an all-water route from the Atlantic Ocean to the Pacific prompted dozens of ships and thousands of men to thread their way around the forbidding islands of Canada's Arctic in search of the elusive prize.

No Arctic explorer was braver or more ambitious than handsome Robert John McClure. That same ambition proved almost fatal in 1851-53 when McClure's ship was trapped in the ice at Mercy Bay and starvation threatened the lives of his crew.

In *Trapped in the Arctic,* Pierre Berton tells the exciting story of McClure's heroism and foolhardiness, and the combination of luck and courage that led him to claim discovery of the fabled North West Passage.